The Complete Anti-Inflammatory Breakfast Cookbook

A complete collection of breakfast Anti-Inflammatory recipes

Natalie Worley

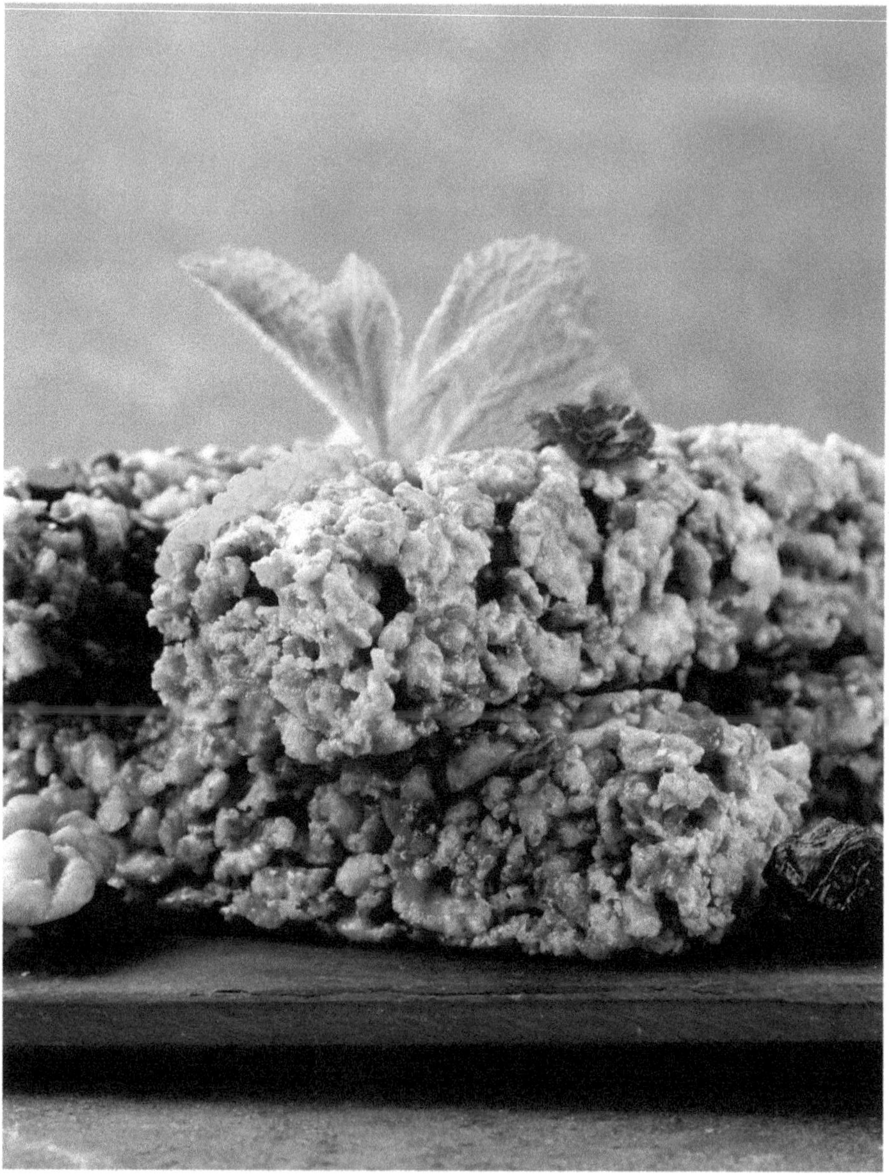

by reading this document, the reader agrees that under no circumstances is the author responsible for any losses, direct or indirect, which are incurred as a result of the use of information contained within this document, including, but not limited to, — errors, omissions, or inaccuracies.

Table of Contents

CRANBERRIES NUTS OATS 6

AVOCADO AND BANANA SMOOTHIE 8

BEET TOMATO SALAD 10

QUINOA WITH STRAWBERRIES AND MAPLE SYRUP 12

CARROTS AND QUINOA MIX... 15

AVOCADO AND TOMATOES SALAD 17

BLACK BEANS, SCALLIONS, AND EGGS MIX...................................20

AVOCADO, PEPPER AND CORN SALAD 22

CHERRY TOMATOES AND EGGS 24

ZUCCHINI ONION SPREAD 27

WATERMELON, ARUGULA AND QUINOA SALAD............................29

PORTUGUESE SALAD...32

TOMATO EGGS..33

VANILLA PEARS 35

STRAWBERRY SALAD 36

SPINACH FRITTATA..38

GRANOLA BARS 40

KALE SALAD 42

QUINOA SALAD...44

SHREDDED CARROT BOWL 46

ITALIAN STYLE SALAD... 47

SPROUTS SALAD 49

CORN BOWL 50

LEMON TOMATOES 51

AVOCADO SALAD 52

BACON AND EGG BREAKFAST CHILI 54

LEMON BLUEBERRY MUFFINS 57

ZUCCHINI MUFFINS...59

ITALIAN SAUSAGE BREAKFAST CUPS 62

ZUCCHINI BREAD WITH WALNUTS...65

BREAKFAST CHICKEN AND EGG 67

EGGS EN COCOTTE 71

BREAKFAST CHOCOLATE ZUCCHINI MUFFINS 73

CAULIFLOWER OATMEAL 76

CHOCOLATE CAULIFLOWER RICE PUDDING 78

MUSHROOM AND CAULIFLOWER RISOTTO 80

COCONUT AND LIME CAULIFLOWER RICE 82

EGGS WITH AVOCADOS AND FETA CHEESE 84

GIANT KETO PANCAKE 86

BREAKFAST BURRITO CASSEROLE 88

BREAKFAST RATATOUILLE 90

SPANISH CHORIZO AND CAULIFLOWER HASH 94

BLT EGG CASSEROLE 96

COCONUT OATMEAL 98

CHEESY TOMATOES 99

BANANA NUT CAKE 101

OLIVES AND KALE 103

CHEESY TURKEY 105

MUSHROOMS AND CHEESE SPREAD 107

CHEESY SAUSAGE BALLS 108

Cranberries Nuts Oats

Prep Time: 10 min | **Cook Time:** 20 min | **Serve:** 4

- 2 tablespoons walnuts, chopped
- 1 tablespoon almonds, chopped
- 1 cup cranberries
- 2 cups almond milk
- ½ cup old fashioned oats
- 1 teaspoon vanilla extract
- 1 teaspoon cinnamon powder

1.In a small pot, combine the cranberries with the oats, the milk, and the other ingredients, toss, bring to a simmer and cook for 20 minutes.

2.Divide the mix into bowls and serve for breakfast.

Nutrition: calories 190, fat 1, fiber 1, carbs 7, protein 6

Avocado and Banana Smoothie

Prep Time: 5 min | **Cook Time:** 0 min | **Serve:** 4

- 2 avocados, pitted, peeled, and chopped
- 1 banana, frozen, peeled, and roughly chopped
- 2 cups baby spinach
- 1 tablespoon almonds, chopped
- 2 cups almond milk, unsweetened

1.In your blender, mix the avocados with the spinach and the other ingredients, pulse well, divide into bowls and serve for breakfast.

Nutrition: calories 519, fat 49.1, fiber 10.7, carbs 22.9, protein 5.7

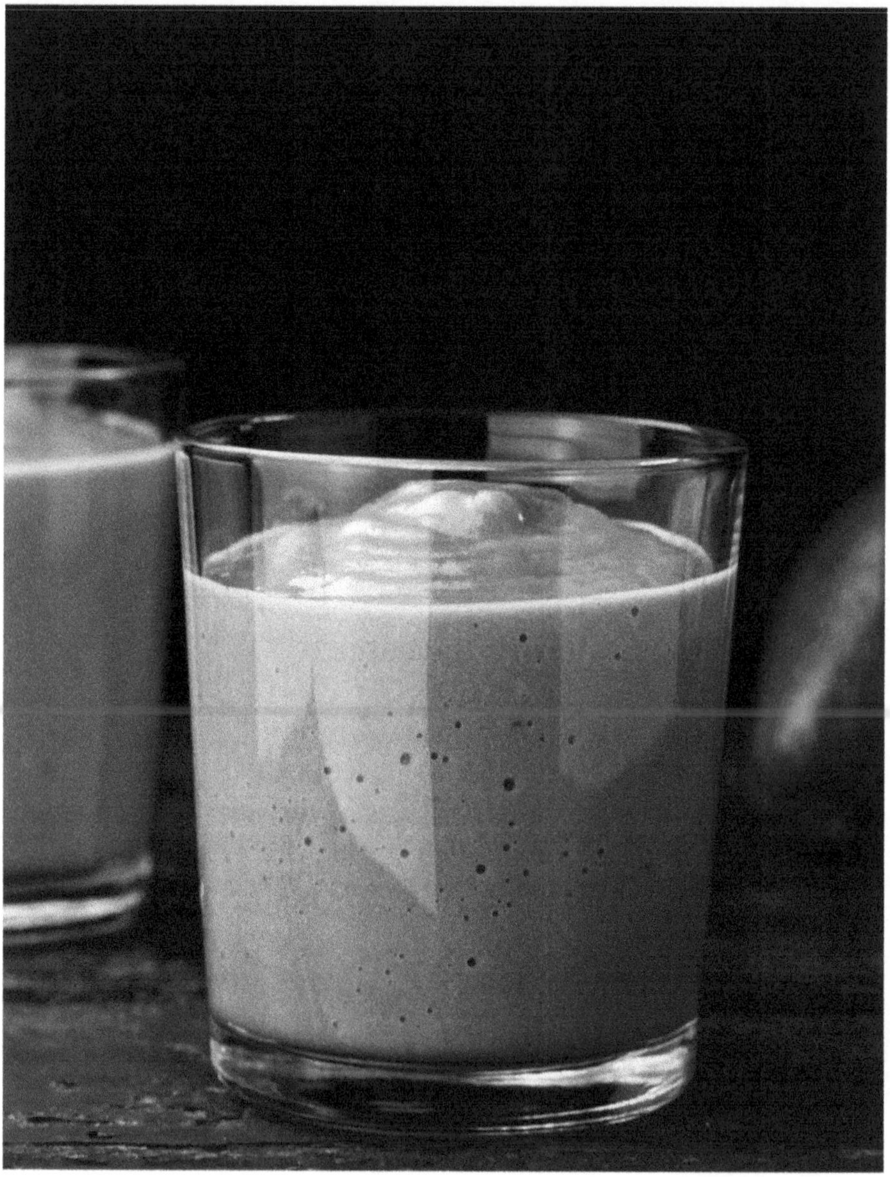

Beet Tomato Salad

Prep Time: 5 min | **Cook Time:** 0 min | **Serve:** 4

- 2 cups beets, baked, peeled, and cubed
- 1 cup baby arugula
- 2 tablespoons olive oil
- 2 shallots, chopped
- 1 cup cherry tomatoes, halved
- Juice of 1 lime
- ¼ inch ginger, grated

1.In a salad bowl, mix the beets with the arugula and the other ingredients, toss, divide into smaller bowls, and serve breakfast.

Nutrition: calories 114, fat 7.3, fiber 2.4, carbs 12/4,

protein 2.2

Quinoa with Strawberries and Maple Syrup

Prep Time: 5 min | **Cook Time:** 0 min | **Serve:** 4

- 2 cups quinoa, cooked
- 1 cup strawberries, halved
- 1 tablespoon maple syrup
- ½ tablespoon lime juice
- 1 teaspoon vanilla extract

1.In a bowl, mix the quinoa with the strawberries and the other ingredients, toss, divide into smaller bowls, and serve breakfast.

Nutrition: calories 170, fat 5.3, fiber 6, carbs 6.8,

protein 5

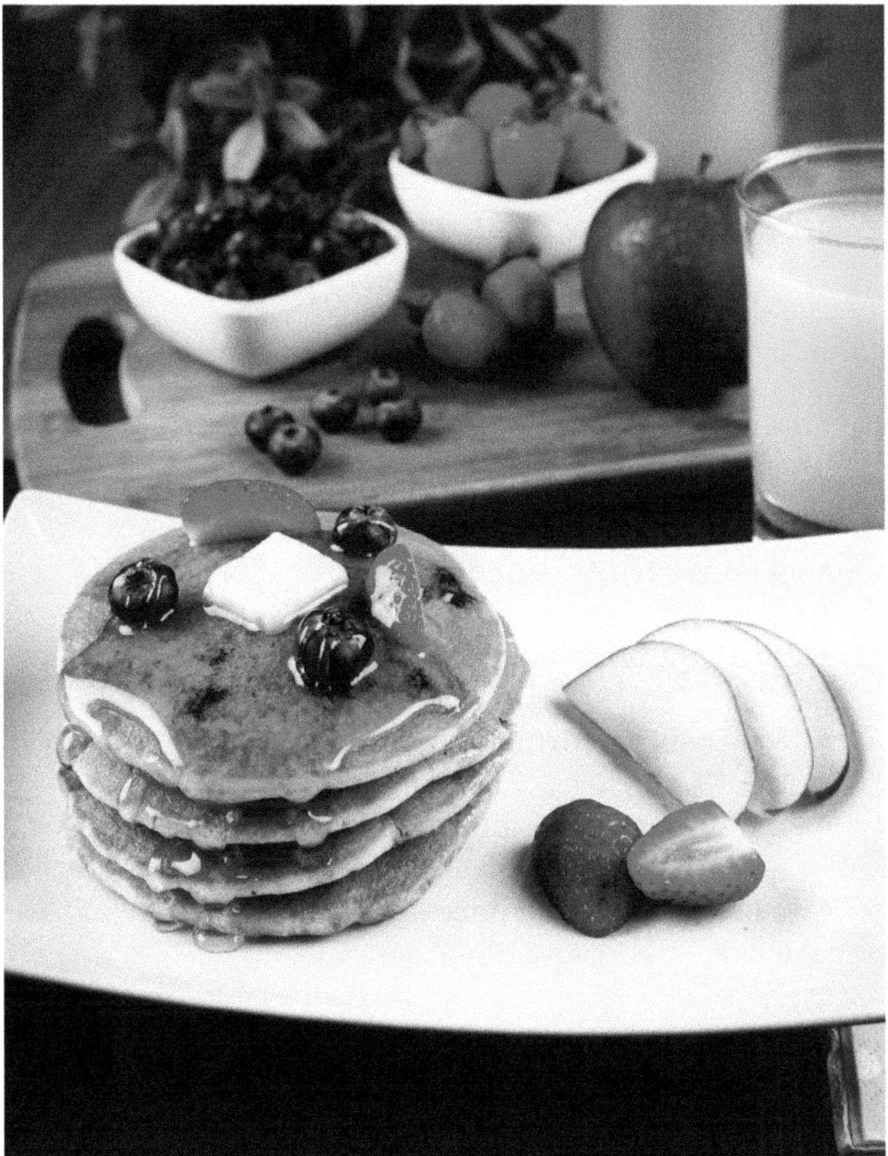

Carrots and Quinoa Mix

Prep Time: 5 min | **Cook Time:** 10 min | **Serve:** 4

- 2 tablespoon maple syrup

- 1 tablespoon almonds, chopped

- 2 cups carrots, shredded

- 1 cup quinoa, cooked

- ¼ teaspoon turmeric powder

- 2 tablespoons sesame seeds

- 1 tablespoon lime juice

1.In a salad bowl, combine the carrots with the quinoa and the other ingredients, toss, divide into ramekins, cook at 350 degrees F for 10 minutes and serve for breakfast.

Nutrition: calories 150, fat 3, fiber 2, carbs 6, protein 8

Avocado and Tomatoes Salad

Prep Time: 5 min | **Cook Time:** 0 min | **Serve:** 4

- 2 cups cherry tomatoes, halved

- 2 scallions, chopped

- 1 tablespoon basil, chopped

- 1 avocado, peeled, pitted and cubed

- 2 tablespoons oregano, chopped

- 1 tablespoon mint, chopped

- 2 tablespoons balsamic vinegar

- 2 tablespoons olive oil

- A pinch of salt and black pepper

1.In a salad bowl, mix the tomatoes with the scallions, the basil, and the other ingredients, toss, divide into smaller bowls and serve for breakfast.

Nutrition: calories 140, fat 2, fiber 3, carbs 6, protein 8

Black Beans, Scallions, and Eggs Mix

Prep Time: 5 min | **Cook Time:** 15 min | **Serve:** 4

- 1 cup canned black beans, drained and rinsed

- 2 green onions, chopped

- 6 eggs, whisked

- ½ teaspoon cumin, ground

- 1 teaspoon chili powder

- 2 scallions, chopped

- 1 tablespoon olive oil

- ½ cup cilantro, chopped

- 2 tablespoons pine nuts

- A pinch of salt and black pepper

1.Heat a pan with the oil over medium heat, add the scallions, green onions, and pine nuts, stir and cook for 2 minutes.

2.Add the beans and cook them for 3 minutes more.

3.Add the eggs and the rest of the ingredients and cook for 10 minutes more, stirring often.

4.Divide everything between plates and serve for breakfast.

Nutrition: calories 140, fat 4, fiber 2, carbs 7, protein 8

Avocado, Pepper and Corn Salad

Prep Time: 5 min | **Cook Time:** 0 min | **Serve:** 4

- 2 avocados, pitted, peeled and cubed
- 1 cup corn
- 2 spring onions, chopped
- 2 red bell peppers, roughly chopped
- 2 tablespoons olive oil
- 1 tablespoon lime juice
- A pinch of salt and black pepper
- 1 tablespoon chives, chopped

1.In a salad bowl, mix the corn with the avocado and the other ingredients, toss well, divide into smaller bowls, and serve breakfast.

Nutrition: calories 140, fat 3, fiber 2, carbs 6, protein 9

Cherry Tomatoes and Eggs

Prep Time: 5 min | **Cook Time:** 15 min | **Serve:** 4

- 2 tablespoons extra-virgin olive oil

- 1 yellow onion, chopped

- 1 cup cherry tomatoes, quartered

- 6 eggs, whisked

- 1 tablespoon basil, chopped

- A pinch of salt and black pepper

1.Heat a pan with the oil over medium-high heat, add the onion and sauté for 5 minutes.

2.Add the eggs and the remaining ingredients, toss, cook for 10 minutes more, divide between plates and serve.

Nutrition: calories 100, fat 1, fiber 2, carbs 2, protein 6

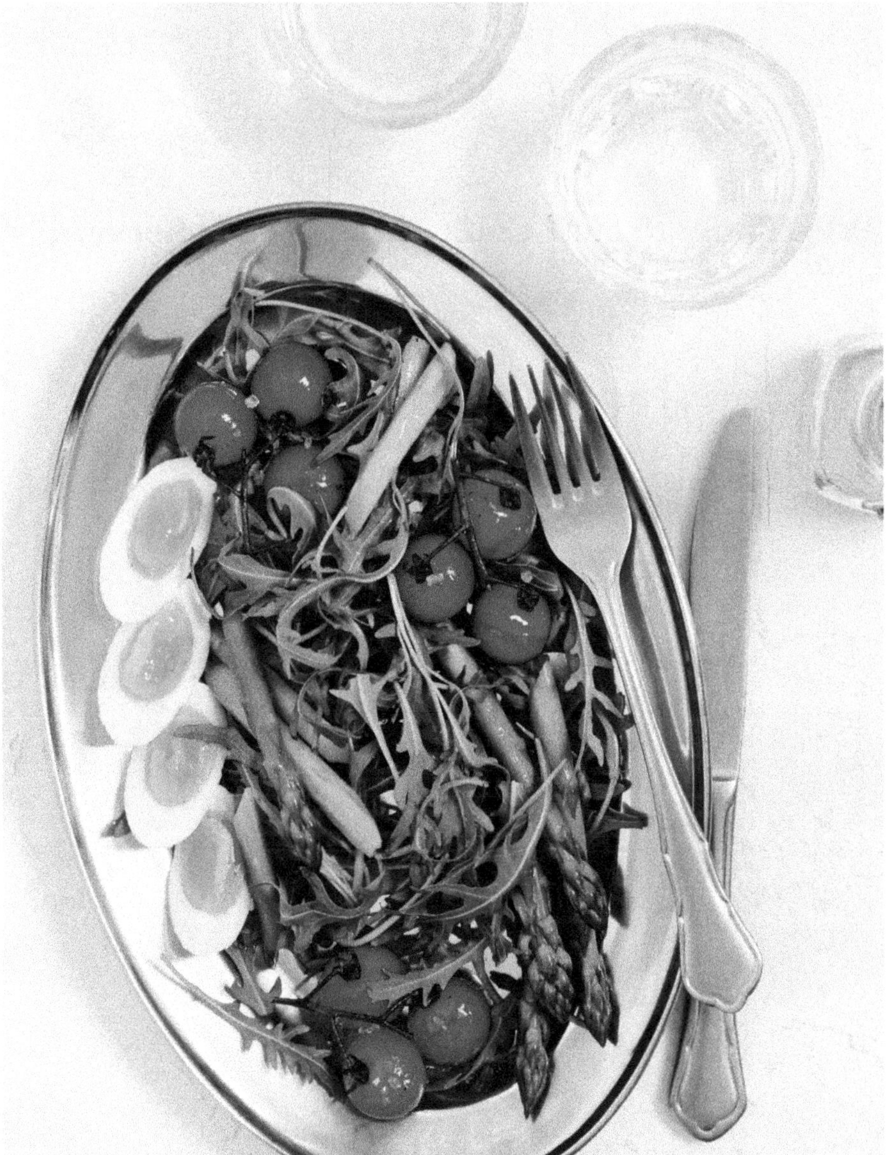

Zucchini Onion Spread

Prep Time: 10 min | **Cook Time:** 15 min | **Serve:** 4

- 1 pound zucchini, chopped

- 1 yellow onion, chopped

- 1 tablespoon coconut cream

- ¼ cup veggie stock

- 2 tablespoons olive oil

- 2 tablespoons lemon juice

- ¼ cup parsley, chopped

- A pinch of salt and black pepper

1.Heat a pan with the oil over medium heat, add the onion, stir and cook for 2 minutes.

2.Add the zucchinis and the other ingredients, stir, bring to a simmer, cook for 13 minutes more, blend using an immersion blender, divide into bowls and serve as a morning spread.

Nutrition: calories 102, fat 8.3, fiber 2.1, carbs 7.1, protein 1.9

Watermelon, Arugula and Quinoa Salad

Prep Time: 10 min | **Cook Time:** 0 min | **Serve:** 4

- ½ teaspoon maple syrup
- 2 tablespoons lemon juice
- 1 tablespoon avocado oil
- 1 cup watermelon, peeled and cubed
- 1 cup baby arugula
- 1 cup quinoa, cooked
- ½ cup basil leaves, chopped

1.In a bowl, mix the watermelon with the arugula and the other ingredients, toss and serve for breakfast.

Nutrition: calories 179, fat 3.2, fiber 3.4, carbs 31.3,

protein 6.5

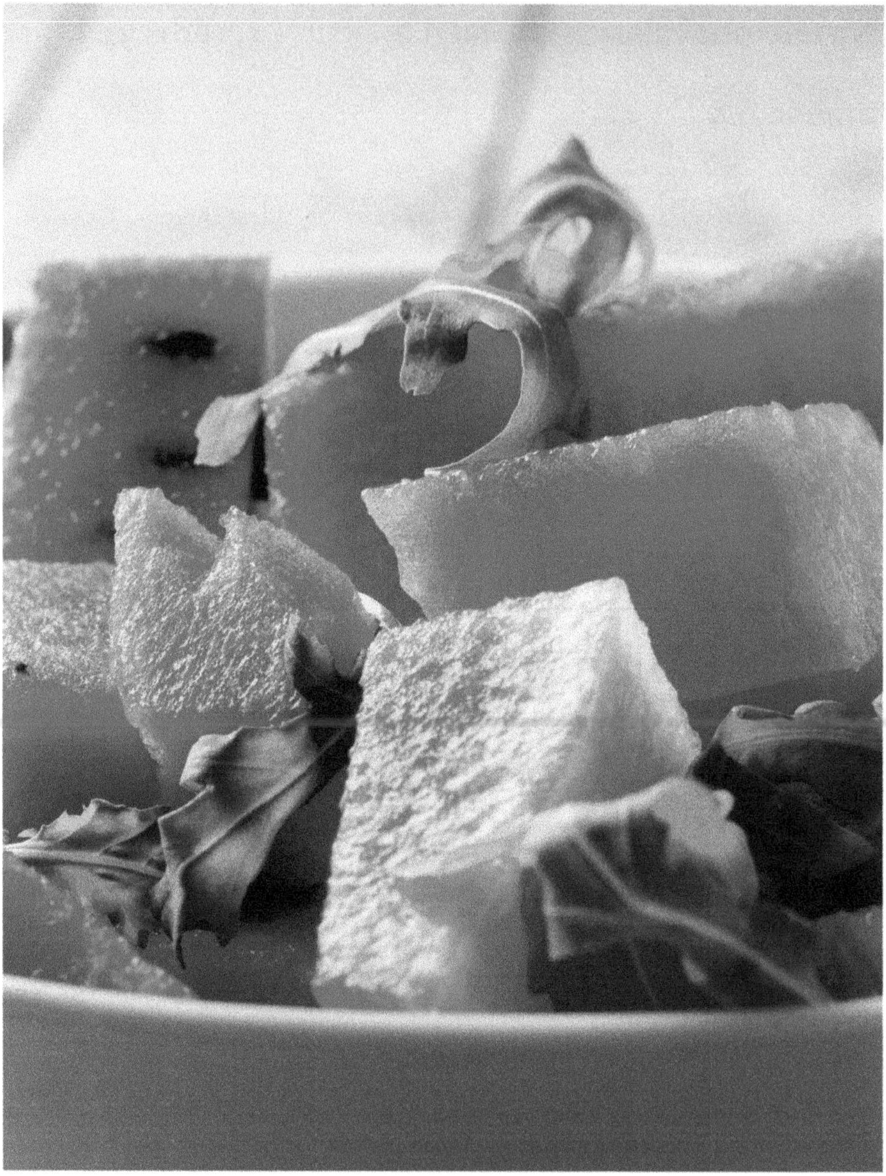

Portuguese Salad

Prep Time: 10 min | **Cook Time:** 0 min | **Serve:** 4

- 3 cups tomatoes, sliced

- 2 red onions, peeled, sliced

- 2 tablespoons olive oil

- ½ teaspoon cayenne pepper

1.Mix tomatoes with red onions, and cayenne pepper.

2.Then top the salad with olive oil and stir it before

serving.

Nutrition: 107 calories,1.8g protein, 10.5g

carbohydrates, 7.4g fat, 2.9g fiber, 0mg cholesterol, 9mg

sodium, 405mg potassium.

Tomato Eggs

Prep Time: 10 min | **Cook Time:** 15 min | **Serve:** 6

- 12 eggs, beaten
- 2 cups tomatoes, chopped
- 2 tablespoons olive oil
- 1 teaspoon dried rosemary
- ½ teaspoon chili powder

1.Preheat the olive oil in the skillet

2.Add tomatoes, dried rosemary, and chili powder.

3.Roast tomatoes for 10 minutes. Stir them from time to time.

4.After this, add eggs, gently stir the meal and cook it for 5 minutes more with the closed lid.

Nutrition: 178 calories,11.6g protein, 29g carbohydrates, 3.3g fat, 13.6g fiber, 327mg cholesterol, 128mg sodium, 266mg potassium.

Vanilla Pears

Prep Time: 10 min | **Cook Time:** 15 min | **Serve:** 4

- 2 cups of rice milk

- 4 pears, chopped

- 1 teaspoon vanilla extract

1.Bring the rice milk to boil.

2.Add vanilla extract and chopped pears.

3.Simmer the meal for 5 minutes on medium heat.

Nutrition: 184 calories,1g protein, 44.4g carbohydrates, 1.3g fat, 6.5g fiber, 0mg cholesterol, 45mg sodium, 278mg potassium.

Strawberry Salad

- 2 oz nuts, chopped

- 1 cup strawberries, sliced

- 2 tablespoons coconut milk

- 1 teaspoon coconut shred

1.Mix nuts with strawberries and coconut shred.

2.Top the salad with coconut milk.

Nutrition: 469 calories,11.5g protein,27.8g carbohydrates, 38.4g fat, 9g fiber, 0mg cholesterol, 386mg sodium, 638mg potassium.

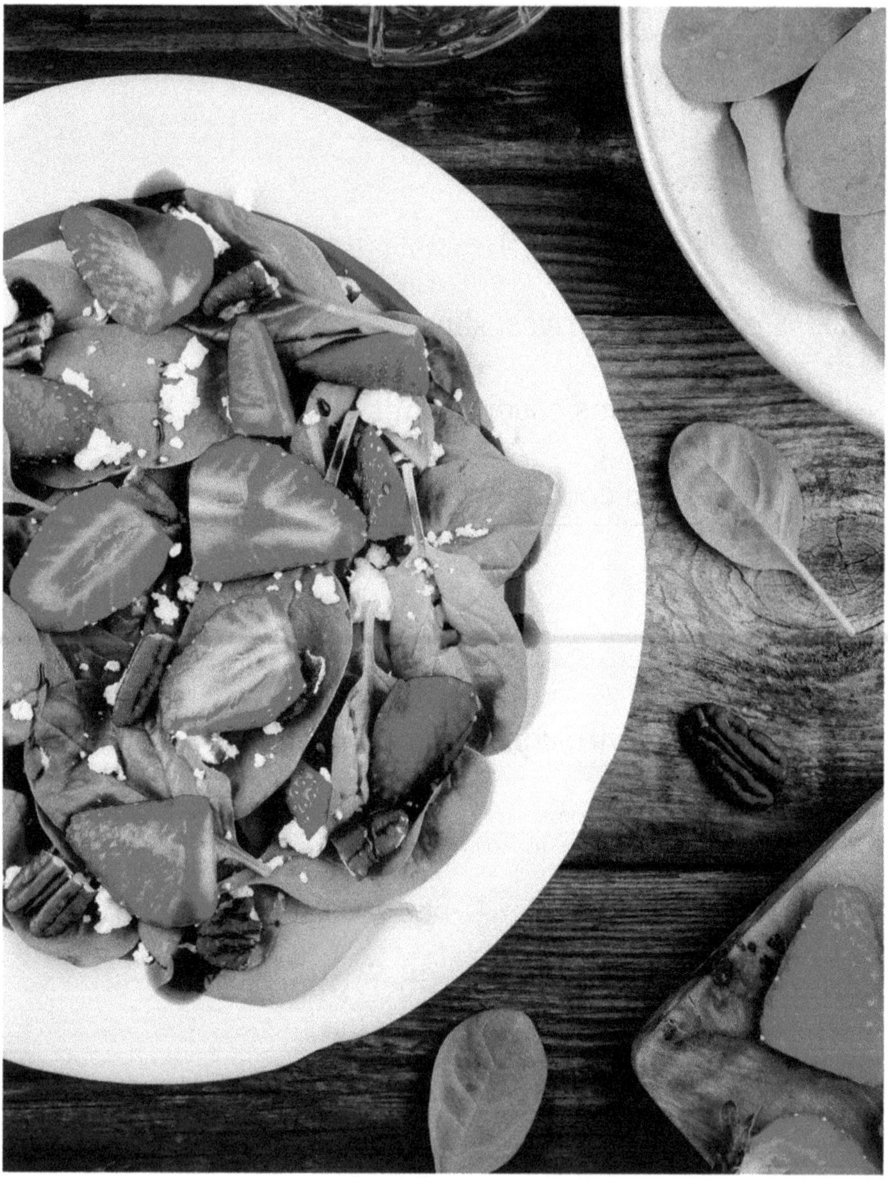

Spinach Frittata

Prep Time: 10 min | **Cook Time:** 30 min | **Serve:** 4

- 2 cups spinach, chopped

- 6 eggs, beaten

- 1 tablespoon cashew butter

- 1 teaspoon chili powder

- ¼ cup coconut cream

1.Mix all ingredients except cashew butter in the mixing bowl.

2.Then grease the baking pan with cashew butter and pour the egg mixture inside.

3.Bake the frittata at 350F for 30 minutes.

Nutrition: 158 calories, 9.9g protein, 29g carbohydrates, 3.3g fat, 12.3g fiber, 246mg cholesterol, 144mg sodium, 246mg potassium.

Granola Bars

Prep Time: 20 min | **Cook Time:** 0 min | **Serve:** 4

- 7 oz pistachios, chopped

- 1 cup dates, pitted

- ½ cup raisins, chopped

- 2 tablespoons chia seeds

1.Mix all ingredients in the bowl.

2.When the mixture is homogenous, transfer it in the

baking paper and flatten it in the shape of a square.

3.Cut the granola into bars.

Nutrition: 479 calories,12.7g protein, 64g

carbohydrates, 25.6g fat, 11.6g fiber, 0mg cholesterol,

269mg sodium, 969mg potassium.

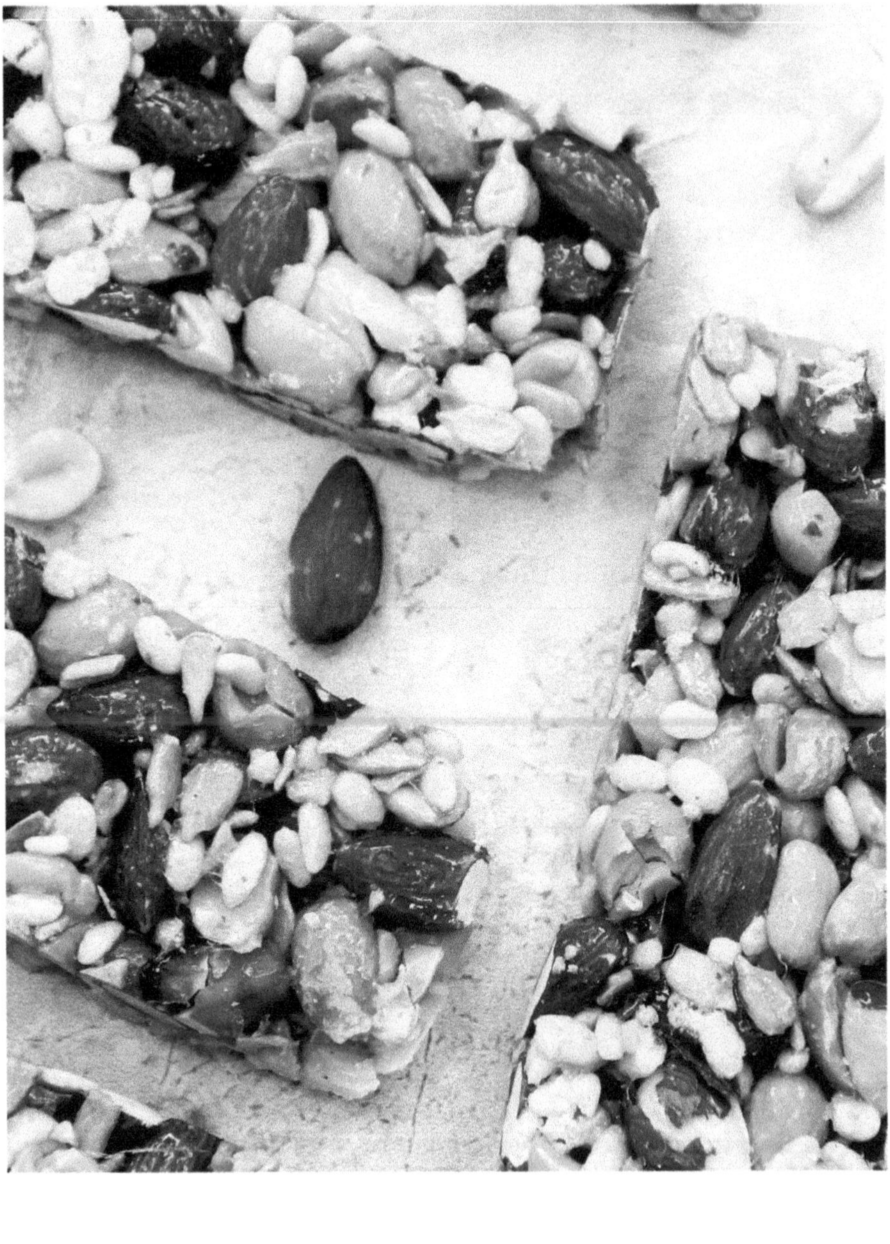

Kale Salad

Prep Time: 10 min | **Cook Time:** 0 min | **Serve:** 4

- 3 cups kale, chopped
- 2 cucumbers, chopped
- ¼ cup fresh parsley, chopped
- 2 tablespoons lemon juice
- ½ teaspoon dried mint
- 3 oz tofu, cubed

1.Mix kale with cucumbers and parsley.

2.Then sprinkle the salad with lemon juice and dried mint.

3.Shake the salad and top it with tofu.

Nutrition: 66 calories,4.4g protein, 11.5g carbohydrates, 1.2g fat, 1.9g fiber, 0mg cholesterol, 31mg sodium, 531mg potassium.

Quinoa Salad

Prep Time: 10 min | **Cook Time:** 0 min | **Serve:** 2

- 2 cups quinoa, cooked
- 1 cup tomatoes, chopped
- 1 cup fresh parsley, chopped
- 1 tablespoon olive oil
- 1 teaspoon lemon juice
- 2 garlic cloves, diced

1.In the salad bowl, mix quinoa with tomatoes, parsley, and garlic cloves.

2.Then add olive oil and lemon juice.

3.Stir the salad.

Nutrition: 718 calories,25.9g protein, 115.5g carbohydrates, 17.8g fat, 14g fiber, 0mg cholesterol, 31mg sodium, 1352mg potassium.

Shredded Carrot Bowl

Prep Time: 10 min | **Cook Time:** 0 min | **Serve:** 4

- 3 cups carrot, shredded
- 3 oz raisins, chopped
- 3 tablespoons lemon juice
- 2 tablespoons olive oil
- 1 tablespoon dried cilantro
- 1 tablespoon raw honey

1.Put all ingredients in the salad bowl and carefully mix.

2.Let the meal rest for at least 5 minutes before serving.

Nutrition: 176 calories,1.5g protein, 29.9g carbohydrates, 7.2g fat, 2.9g fiber, 0mg cholesterol, 62mg sodium, 441mg potassium.

Italian Style Salad

Prep Time: 10 min | **Cook Time:** 0 min **Serve:** 4

- 1 tablespoon Italian seasonings

- 2 tablespoons olive oil

- 2 oz Parmesan, grated

- 2 oz olives, chopped

- 1 cup tomatoes, chopped

- 1 cup cucumbers, chopped

1.Mix olives with tomatoes and cucumbers.

2.Then sprinkle the salad with Italian seasonings and olive oil.

3.Shake the salad.

4.Top it with parmesan.

Nutrition: 145 calories,5.3g protein, 4.5g carbohydrates, 12.7g fat, 1.1g fiber, 13mg cholesterol, 259mg sodium, 148mg potassium.

Sprouts Salad

Prep Time: 10 min | **Cook Time:** 0 min | **Serve:** 4

- 1 red onion, sliced

- 2 cups bean sprouts

- 1 cup fresh cilantro, chopped

- 1 tablespoon lemon juice

- 1 teaspoon dried rosemary

- 1 tablespoon olive oil

1.Put all ingredients in the salad bowl.

2.Shake the salad well.

Nutrition: 71 calories,4.3g protein, 6.8g carbohydrates, 4.1g fat, 0.9g fiber, 0mg cholesterol, 9mg sodium, 241mg potassium.

Corn Bowl

Prep Time: 10 min | **Cook Time:** 0 min | **Serve:** 4

- 10 oz corn kernels, cooked

- 1 cup tomatoes, chopped

- 1 tablespoon fresh dill, chopped

- 1 tablespoon plain yogurt

- ½ cup radish, chopped

1.Mix tomatoes with fresh dill, plain yogurt, and radish.

2.Then add corn kernels, gently stir the meal.

Nutrition: 345 calories,13.4g protein, 75.5g carbohydrates, 4.7g fat, 11.4g fiber, 0mg cholesterol, 70mg sodium, 1215mg potassium.

Lemon Tomatoes

Prep Time: 10 min | **Cook Time:** 0 min | **Serve:** 6

- 4 cups arugula, chopped

- 4 cups tomatoes, chopped

- 2 tablespoons olive oil

- 3 tablespoons lemon juice

- 1 teaspoon lemon zest, grated

1.Put tomatoes and arugula in the salad bowl.

2.Add lemon juice, olive oil, and lemon zest.

3.Stir the meal gently before serving.

Nutrition: 67 calories,1.5g protein, 5.4g carbohydrates, 5.1g fat, 1.7g fiber, 0mg cholesterol, 11mg sodium, 344mg potassium.

Avocado Salad

Prep Time: 10 min | **Cook Time:** 0 min | **Serve:** 4

- 3 tomatoes, roughly chopped
- 2 avocados, pitted and chopped
- 1 cup parsley, chopped
- 1 teaspoon cayenne pepper
- ½ teaspoon dried rosemary
- 2 tablespoons olive oil

1. In the salad bowl, mix tomatoes with avocados, parsley, and dried rosemary.

2. Then sprinkle the salad with olive oil and cayenne pepper. Gently shake the salad.

Nutrition: 289 calories,3.2g protein, 13.5g carbohydrates, 27g fat, 8.5g fiber, 0mg cholesterol, 19mg sodium, 800mg potassium.

Bacon and Egg Breakfast Chili

Prep Time: 25 minutes | **Serve:** 8

- 1 pound of breakfast sausage, thawed and roughly chopped
- ½ pound of bacon, chopped
- 6 large organic eggs
- 1 medium white onion, finely chopped
- 2 tablespoons of olive oil
- 1 (28-ounce can of diced tomatoes with green chiles 2-3 cups of homemade low-sodium chicken broth 2 teaspoons of smoked paprika or regular paprika 2 teaspoons of chili powder
- 2 teaspoons of garlic powder
- 1 teaspoon of onion powder

- 1 teaspoon of fine sea salt Avocado slices

1.Press the "Sauté" function on your Instant Pot and add the bacon. Cook until brown and crispy, stirring occasionally. 2.Transfer the bacon to a plate lined with paper towels.

3.Add the breakfast sausage and onions to the bacon grease and cook until the sausage has browned.

4.Add the remaining ingredients except for the eggs to your

5. Instant Pot. Lock the lid and cook at high pressure for 10 minutes.

6.When the cooking is done, naturally release the pressure and remove the lid

7.Meanwhile, fry or scramble your eggs on a stovetop skillet the way you like.

8.You can skip this step if you only want to use your

Instant Pot.

9.Once everything is done, scoop the breakfast chili onto

bowls and top with eggs, bacon, and avocado slices.

Nutrition: Calories: 441, Fat: 34.9g, Net Carb: 3.4g,

Protein: 26.5g

Lemon Blueberry Muffins

Prep Time: 15 minutes | **Serve:** 6

- 2 cups of almond flour
- 1 cup of heavy whipping cream
- 2 large organic eggs, beaten
- ¼ cup of coconut butter or ghee, melt
- 1 tablespoon of granulated erythritol or other keto-friendly sweeteners
- ½ cup of fresh or frozen blueberries
- 1 teaspoon of fresh lemon zest
- 1 teaspoon of lemon extract 1/8 teaspoon of fine sea salt

1.In a large bowl, add all the ingredients and gently stir until well combined.

2.Grease 6 silicone muffin cups with nonstick cooking spray

Divide and add the muffin batter into each muffin cup.

3.Add 1 cup of water and a trivet inside your Instant Pot. Place the muffin cup on top of the trivet and cover with aluminum foil.

4.Lock the lid and cook at high pressure for 8 minutes. When the timer beeps, naturally release the pressure for 10 minutes. Carefully remove the lid.

5.Check if the muffins are cooked by using a toothpick.

Nutrition: Calories: 220, Fat: 21g, Net Carb: 3g, Protein: 4g

Zucchini Muffins

Prep Time: 15 minutes | **Serve:** 6

- 1 large zucchini, finely grated
- 6 medium bacon slices, chopped
- 4 large organic eggs
- ½ cup of heavy whipping cream
- 1 cup of shredded cheddar cheese
- 1 cup of almond flour
- 4 tablespoons of flax meal
- ½ cup of parmesan cheese, finely grated
- 1 tablespoon of dried Italian herbs
- 2 teaspoons of onion powder
- 1 teaspoon of baking powder
- ½ teaspoon of garlic powder

- ½ teaspoon of fine sea salt

- ½ teaspoon of freshly cracked black pepper

1.Grease 6 silicone muffin cups with nonstick cooking spray.

2.In a large bowl, add all the ingredients and gently stir until well combined.

3.Divide and spoon the batter into each muffin cup.

4.Add 2 cups of water and a trivet inside your Instant Pot. Place the muffin cups on top and cover with aluminum foil.

5.Lock the lid and cook at high pressure for 10 minutes. When the cooking is done, naturally release the pressure for 10 minutes. Carefully remove the lid and check if the muffins are done.

Nutrition: Calories: 216, Fat: 17g, Net Carb: 2.7g, Protein: 12.9g

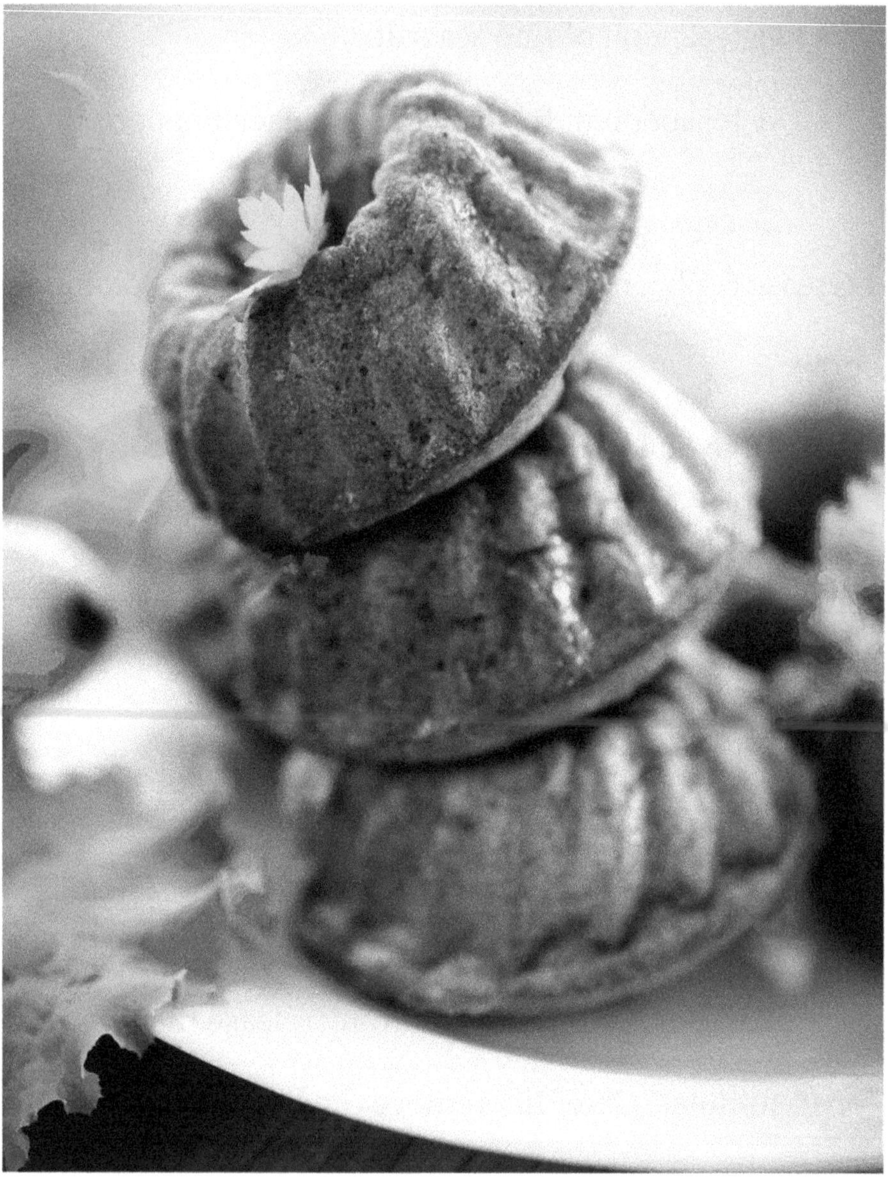

Italian Sausage Breakfast Cups

Prep Time: 20 minutes | **Serve:** 4

- 1 pound of Italian sausage links, cut into bite-sized pieces
- 4 large eggs, beaten
- 1 medium yellow or white onion, finely chopped
- 1 teaspoon of fine sea salt
- 1 teaspoon of freshly cracked black pepper
- ½ cup of mushrooms, finely chopped
- ½ cup of broccoli florets, chopped
- ½ cup of spinach, roughly chopped
- 1 tablespoon of fresh parsley, finely chopped
- 2 tablespoons of olive oil

1.Press the "Sauté" function on your Instant Pot and add the olive oil. Once hot, add the onions, mushrooms, and broccoli. Cook until softened, stirring occasionally. Remove and set aside.

2.Add the Italian sausage and cook until brown, stirring occasionally. Turn off "Sauté" function on your Instant Pot.

3.In a large bowl, add the vegetables, cooked Italian sausage and remaining ingredients. Stir until well combined. Divide the mixture between 6 silicon muffin cups or greased ramekins.

4.Add 1 cup of water and a trivet inside your Instant Pot. Place the muffin cups on top and lock the lid. Cook at high pressure for 10 minutes.

5.When the cooking is done, naturally release the pressure and carefully remove the lid.

Nutrition: Calories: 288, Fat: 23g, Net Carb: 1g,

Protein: 16.5g

Zucchini Bread with Walnuts

Prep Time: 1 hour and 15 minutes | **Serve:** 16

- 3 large organic eggs, beaten
- ½ cup of extra-virgin olive oil
- 1 cup of zucchini, finely grated
- ½ cup of walnuts, chopped
- 1 teaspoon of pure vanilla extract
- 2 ½ cups of almond flour
- ½ cup of erythritol or other keto-friendly sweeteners
- ½ teaspoon of fine sea salt
- 1 teaspoon of baking soda or baking powder
- ¼ teaspoon of grated ginger
- 1 teaspoon of cinnamon

1.In a large bowl, add all the ingredients and gently stir until well blended.

2.Grease a 7-inch pan that fits inside your Instant Pot with nonstick cooking spray.

3.Add the bread batter to the pan and cover with aluminum foil.

4.Add 1 cup of water and place a trivet inside your Instant Pot. Place the pan on top of the trivet.

5.Lock the lid and cook at high pressure for 55 minutes. When the cooking is done, naturally release the pressure for 10 minutes. Carefully remove the lid. Unfold the aluminum foil and allow it to cool.

Nutrition: Calories: 200, Fat: 19g, Net Carb: 3g, Protein: 6g

Breakfast Chicken and Egg

Prep Time: 30 minutes | **Serve:** 6

- 1 pound of boneless, skinless chicken breasts

- 6 large organic eggs

- 2 tablespoons of extra-virgin olive oil

- 1 large onion, finely chopped

- 1 cup of water

- ½ cup of cauliflower rice

- 2 tablespoons of fresh parsley, finely chopped

- 1 teaspoon of fine sea salt

- 1 teaspoon of freshly cracked black pepper

1.Press the "Sauté" function on your Instant Pot and add the olive oil. Once hot, add the onions and cook until fragrant, stirring occasionally. Remove and set aside.

2.Add the chicken and cook for 4 minutes per side or until brown.

3.Pour in 1 cup of water and lock the lid. Cook at high pressure for 15 minutes.

4.When the cooking is done, naturally release the pressure and remove the lid.

5.Transfer the chicken to a cutting board and shred using two forks.

6.In a large bowl, add the shredded chicken, eggs, onions, cauliflower rice, fresh parsley, salt, and black pepper. Stir until well combined.

7.Grease an oven-proof dish that fits inside your Instant Pot. Add the egg mixture and cover with foil.

8.Place a trivet inside your Instant Pot and place the dish on top. Lock the lid and cook at high pressure for another 8 minutes.

9.When the cooking is done, naturally release the pressure and remove the lid. Serve and enjoy!

Nutrition: Calories: 275, Fat: 13g, Net Carb: 2g, Protein: 35g

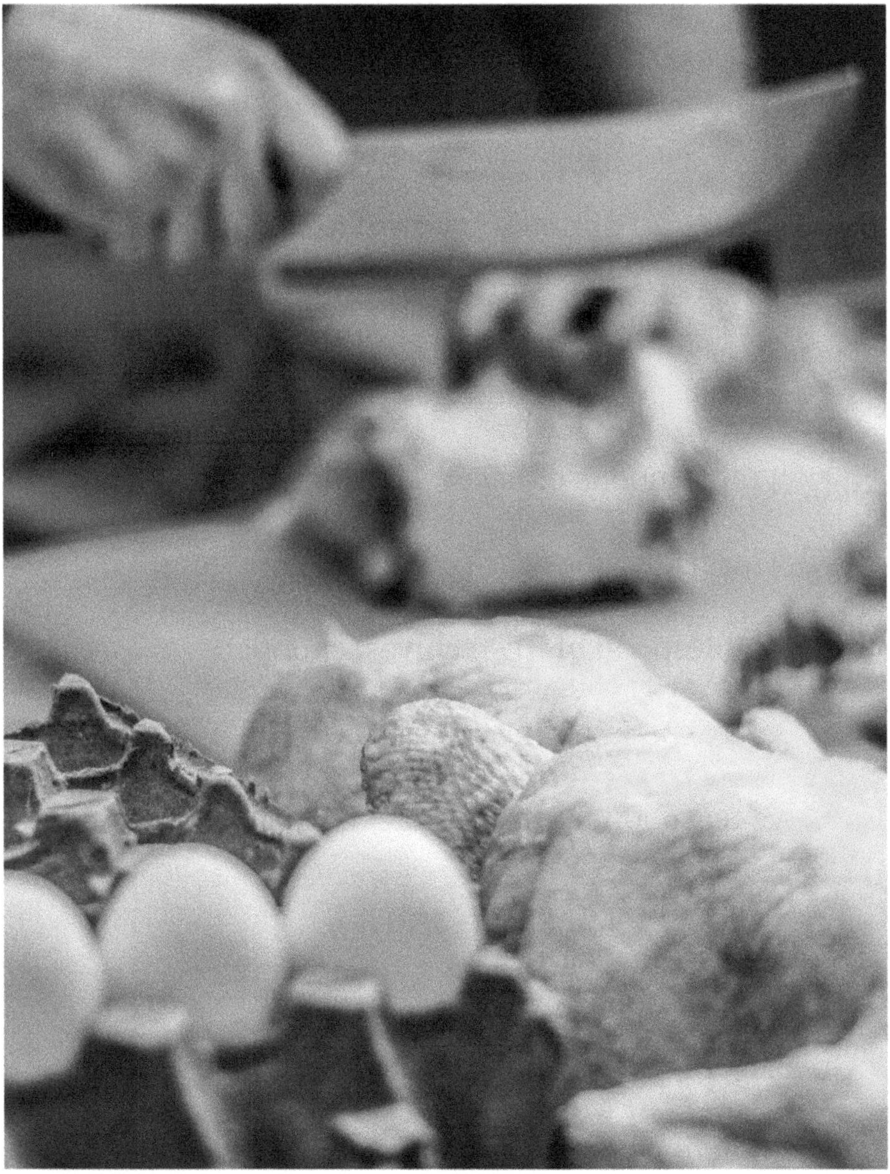

Eggs en Cocotte

Prep Time: 20 minutes | **Serve:** 3

- 3 tablespoons of unsalted butter
- 3 tablespoons of heavy whipping cream
- 3 large organic eggs
- 1 tablespoon of fresh chives, chopped
- ½ teaspoon of fine sea salt
- ½ teaspoon of freshly cracked black pepper
- 1 cup of water

1.Grease 3 ramekins with unsalted butter and add 1 tablespoon of heavy whipping cream into each one.

2.Crack an egg into each ramekin and sprinkle with fresh chives, salt, and black pepper.

3.Add 1 cup of water and a trivet inside your Instant Pot. Place the ramekins on top of the trivet and cover with aluminum foil. Lock the lid and cook at low pressure for 2 minutes.

4.When the timer beeps, naturally release the pressure and carefully remove the lid.

Nutrition: Calories: 420, Fat: 44.5g, Net Carbs: 0.8g, Protein: 6.2g

Breakfast Chocolate Zucchini Muffins

Prep Time: 40 minutes | **Serve:** Around 24 muffin bites

- 2 large organic eggs
- ½ cup of coconut oil, melted
- 2 teaspoons of pure vanilla extract
- 1 tablespoon of unsalted butter
- 3 tablespoons of unsweetened cocoa powder
- 1 cup of almond flour
- ½ teaspoon of baking soda or baking powder
- 1 cup of evaporated cane juice
- 1 cup of water
- ½ teaspoon of ground cinnamon

- 1 cup of finely grated zucchini

- 1/3 cup of mini chocolate chips

- A small pinch of fine sea salt

1.In a large bowl, add all the ingredients one by one and gently stir until well blended.

2.Fill silicone muffin cups with the batter.

3.Add 1 cup of water and a trivet inside your Instant Pot. Layer the muffins on top of the trivet. Cover with aluminum foil.

4.Lock the lid and cook at high pressure for 8 minutes. When the cooking is done, naturally release the pressure and remove the lid.

5.Remove the muffins and check if done using toothpicks.

Nutrition: Calories: 71, Fat: 6.8g, Net Carbs: 1.8g,

Protein: 1g

Cauliflower Oatmeal

Prep Time: 15 minutes | **Serve:** 1

- 1 cup of fine cauliflower rice

- ½ cup of coconut cream

- ½ teaspoon of organic ground cinnamon ¼ teaspoon of granulated erythritol

- ½ tablespoon of peanut butter

- A small pinch of fine sea salt

1.Add all the ingredients except for the peanut butter and stir until well combined.

2.Lock the lid and cook at high pressure for 2 minutes.

3.When the cooking is done, naturally release the pressure and remove the lid. Transfer to bowls and top with peanut butter.

Nutrition: Calories: 140, Fat: 7g, Net Carbs: 8g,

Protein: 7g

Chocolate Cauliflower Rice Pudding

Prep Time: 16 minutes | **Serve:** 2

- 2 cups of fine cauliflower rice

- 1 cup of heavy whipping cream

- 1/3 cup of granulated erythritol or other keto-friendly sweeteners

- 1 to 2 egg whites

- 1 teaspoon of pure vanilla extract

- 3 tablespoons of unsweetened cocoa powder

- A small pinch of fine sea salt

1.Add all the ingredients and stir until well combined.

2.Lock the lid and cook at high pressure for 2 minutes. When the cooking is done, naturally release the pressure and carefully remove the lid.

Nutrition: Calories: 313, Fat: 27.7g, Net Carbs: 5g, Protein: 10g

Mushroom and Cauliflower Risotto

Prep Time: 25 minutes | **Serve:** 4

- 1 medium cauliflower head, cut into florets

- 1 pound of shiitake mushrooms, sliced

- 3 medium garlic cloves, peeled and minced

- 2 tablespoons of coconut aminos

- 1 cup of homemade low-sodium chicken stock

- 1 cup of full-fat coconut milk

- 1 tablespoon of coconut oil, melted

- 1 small onion, finely chopped

- 2 tablespoons of almond flour

- ¼ cup of nutritional yeast

1.Press the "Sauté" function on your Instant Pot and add the coconut oil.

2.Once hot, add the onions, mushrooms, and garlic. Sauté for 5 minutes or until softened, stirring occasionally.

3.Add the remaining ingredients except for the almond flour. Lock the lid and cook at high pressure for 2 minutes.

4.When the cooking is done, naturally release the pressure and remove the lid.

5.Sprinkle the almond flour over the risotto and stir to thicken.

Nutrition: Calories: 230, Fat: 18.5g, Net Carbs: 8g, Protein: 7.5g

Coconut and Lime Cauliflower Rice

Prep Time: 15 minutes | **Serve:** 4

- 1 large cauliflower, chopped

- 2 tablespoons of extra-virgin olive oil

- 1 large yellow onion, finely chopped

- 3 medium garlic cloves, peeled and minced

- 1 (15-ounce can of full-fat coconut milk

- 1 medium lime, zest, and juice

- ½ teaspoon of fine sea salt

- ¼ teaspoon of freshly cracked black pepper

1.Add the cauliflowers to a food processor and pulse until they resemble rice-like consistency.

2.Press the "Sauté" function on your Instant Pot and add the olive oil. Once hot, add the onions and garlic. Sauté for 2 to 3 minutes or until fragrant, stirring occasionally.

3.Add the remaining ingredients and lock the lid. Cook at high pressure for 3 minutes.

4.When the cooking is done, quickly release the pressure and remove the lid.

Nutrition: Calories: 160, Fat: 11g, Net Carbs: 6g, Protein: 5g

Eggs with Avocados and Feta Cheese

Prep Time: 10 minutes | **Serve:** 2

- 4 large organic eggs
- 1 large avocado, peeled and cut into 12 slices
- 2 tablespoons of crumbled feta cheese
- 1 tablespoon of fresh parsley, finely chopped
- ½ teaspoon of fine sea salt
- ½ teaspoon of freshly cracked black pepper
- Grease 2 gratin dishes with nonstick cooking spray.

1.Arrange 6 avocado slices into each gratin dish. Crack 2 eggs into each dish.

2.Sprinkle with crumbled feta cheese, fresh parsley, salt, and black pepper.

3.Wrap with aluminum foil.

4.Add 1 cup of water and a trivet inside your Instant Pot. Place the gratin dish on top of the trivet.

5.Lock the lid and cook at high pressure for 4 minutes. When the cooking is done, quick release or naturally release the pressure. Carefully remove the lid and check if the eggs are done.

Nutrition: Calories: 362, Fat: 30g, Net Carb: 4g, Protein: 16g

Giant Keto Pancake

Prep Time: 50 minutes | **Serve:** 6

- 2 cups of almond flour or coconut flour

- 2 teaspoons of baking powder

- 2 tablespoons of granulated erythritol or another keto-friendly sweetener

- 2 large organic eggs

- 1 ½ cup of unsweetened almond milk or coconut milk

1.In a large bowl, add all the ingredients and stir until well combined.

2.Grease a springform pan with nonstick cooking spray and add the pancake batter.

3.Add 1 cup of water and a trivet inside your Instant Pot.

Place the springform pan on top of the trivet.

4.Lock the lid and cook at low pressure for 45 minutes.

When the cooking is done, remove the lid and allow the

pancake to cool.

Nutrition: Calories: 280, Fat: 24g, Net Carbs: 1g,

Protein: 9g

Breakfast Burrito Casserole

Prep Time: 25 minutes | **Serve:** 6

- 4 large organic eggs

- 1 cup of cheddar cheese, cubed

- ¼ cup of white or yellow onion, finely chopped

- 1 medium jalapeno, finely chopped

- 1 cup of cooked ham, cut into cubes ½ teaspoon of fine sea salt

- ½ teaspoon of freshly cracked black pepper ½ teaspoon of chili powder

- Lettuce leaves

1.In a large bowl, add all the ingredients and stir until well combined.

2.Grease a springform pan or a round metal bowl with nonstick cooking spray.

3.Add the egg mixture.

4.Add 1 cup of water and a trivet inside your Instant Pot. Place the pan on top of the trivet and cover with aluminum foil.

5.Lock the lid and cook at high pressure for 12 minutes. When the cooking is done, naturally release the pressure and remove the lid. Remove the pan and spoon the egg mixture onto lettuce leaves. Top with salsa and avocado slices.

Nutrition: Calories: 165, Fat: 11.5g, Net Carbs: 1.5g, Protein: 13g

Breakfast Ratatouille

Prep Time: 30 minutes | **Serve:** 6

- 12 large organic eggs

- ¼ cup of extra-virgin olive oil

- 1 medium yellow onion, finely chopped

- 6 medium garlic cloves, peeled and finely minced

- 1 (28-ounce can of plum tomatoes, drained

- 1 medium eggplant, chopped

- 1 zucchini, sliced

- 1 medium yellow bell pepper, seeded and chopped

- 1 tablespoon of capers, chopped

- 1 tablespoon of red wine vinegar

- 2 teaspoons of fresh thyme, finely chopped

- 1 teaspoon of fresh oregano, finely chopped

- 3 tablespoons of fresh basil, finely chopped

- 3 tablespoons of fresh parsley, finely chopped

1.Press the "Sauté" function on your Instant Pot and add olive oil and onions.

2.Sauté for 4 minutes or until slightly softened, stirring occasionally.

3.Add the garlic and herbs. Sauté until fragrant, stirring occasionally.

4.Add the tomatoes, eggplant, bell peppers, and zucchini. Stir until well combined.

5.Lock the lid and cook at high pressure for 5 minutes. When the cooking is done, quickly release the pressure and remove the lid.

6.Stir in the capers and red wine vinegar.

7.In a small skillet over medium-high heat, add the

vegetables. Make small cavities and crack eggs into the

cavity. Cover and allow the eggs to cook through.

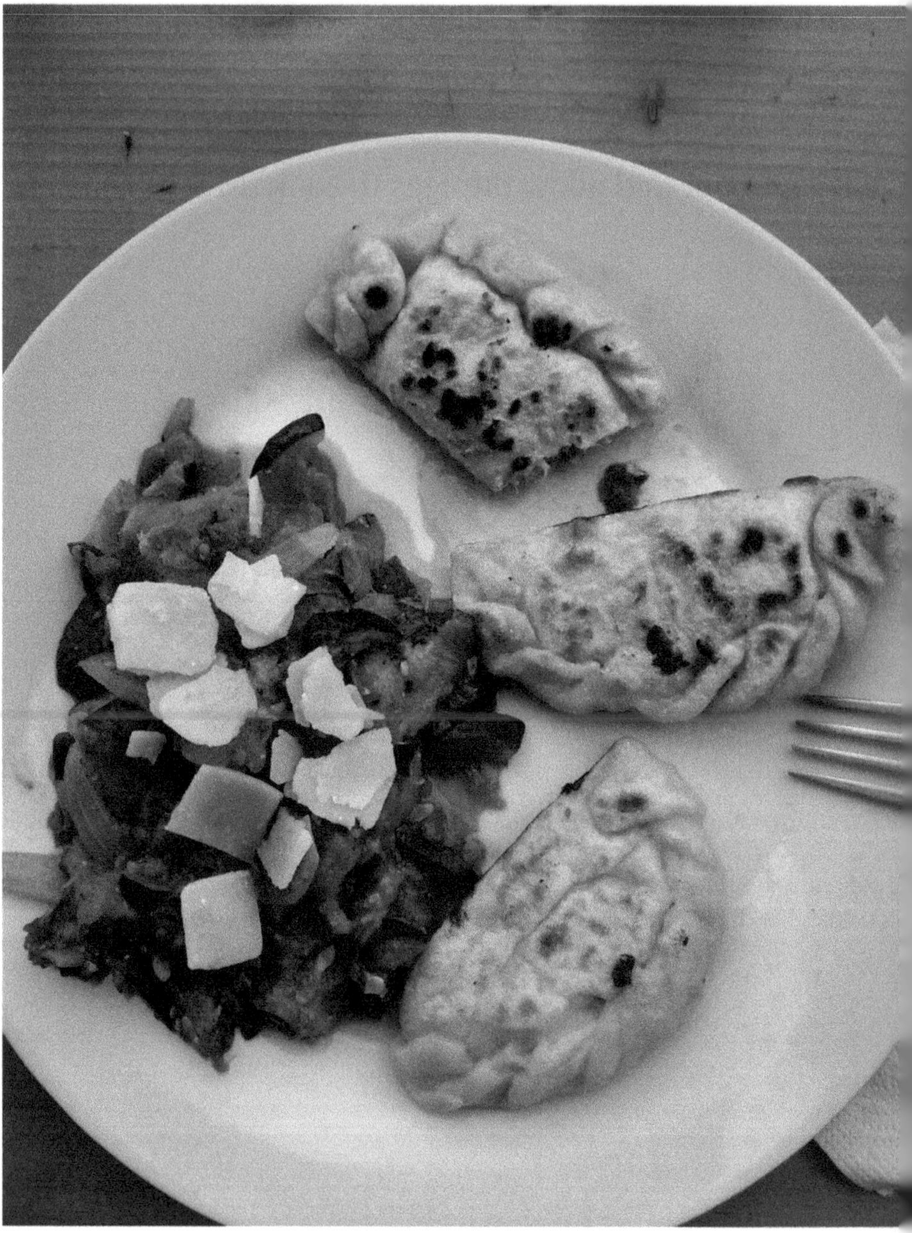

Spanish Chorizo and Cauliflower Hash

Prep Time: 20 minutes | **Serve:** 4

- 1 pound of cauliflower florets, cut into florets
- 1 tablespoon of extra-virgin olive oil
- 1 medium sweet potato, cut into bite-sized pieces
- 1 pound of chorizo sausage, crumbled
- 1 large onion, finely chopped
- 2 medium garlic cloves, peeled and minced
- 3 tablespoons of fresh rosemary, finely chopped
- 3 tablespoons of fresh basil, finely chopped
- 1 teaspoon of fine sea salt
- 1 teaspoon of freshly cracked black pepper
- ½ cup of homemade low-sodium vegetable stock

1.Press the "Sauté" function on your Instant Pot and add the olive oil. Once hot, add the onions and garlic. Sauté for 2 minutes or until softened, stirring occasionally.

2.Add the sweet potato pieces, chorizo sausage, and cauliflower. Sauté for 3 minutes, stirring occasionally.

3.Add the remaining ingredients and stir until well combined.

4.Pour in the vegetable stock and lock the lid. Cook at high pressure for 10 minutes. When the cooking is done, naturally release the pressure and remove the lid. Serve and enjoy!

Nutrition: Calories: 550, Fat: 35g, Net Carbs: 12g, Protein: 23g

BLT Egg Casserole

Prep Time: 30 minutes | **Serve:** 4

- 6 large organic eggs

- 6 medium slices of bacon, chopped

- 1 medium Roma tomato, sliced

- ½ cup of cheddar cheese, shredded

- 2 green onions, thinly sliced

- ½ cup of heavy whipping cream

- ½ cup of fresh spinach

- 1 teaspoon of fine sea salt

- 1 teaspoon of freshly cracked black pepper

1.In a large bowl, add all the ingredients and stir until well combined.

2.Grease a large springform pan with nonstick cooking spray and add the egg mixture.

3.Add 1 cup of water and place a trivet inside your Instant Pot. Place the springform pan on top of the trivet and cover with aluminum foil.

4.Lock the lid and cook at high pressure for 13 minutes.

5.When the cooking is done, naturally release the pressure for 10 minutes, then quickly release the remaining pressure. Remove the lid.

Nutrition: Calories: 360, Fat: 29g, Net Carbs: 2g, Protein: 23g

Coconut Oatmeal

Prep Time: 20 minutes | **Serve:** 4

- 2 cups almond milk

- 1 cup coconut; shredded

- 2 tsp. vanilla extract

- 2 tsp. stevia

1.In a pan that fits your air fryer, mix all the ingredients, stir well, introduce the pan in the machine and cook at 360°F for 15 minutes

2.Divide into bowls and serve for breakfast.

Nutrition: Calories: 201; Fat: 13g; Fiber: 2g; Carbs: 4g; Protein: 7g

Cheesy Tomatoes

Prep Time: 20 minutes | **Serve:** 4

- 1 lb. cherry tomatoes; halved

- 1 cup mozzarella; shredded

- 1 tsp. basil; chopped.

- Cooking spray

- Salt and black pepper to taste.

1.Grease the tomatoes with the cooking spray, season with salt and pepper, sprinkle the mozzarella on top, place them all in your air fryer's basket, cook at 330°F for 15 minutes

2.Divide into bowls, sprinkle the basil on top, and serve.

Nutrition: Calories: 140; Fat: 7g; Fiber: 3g; Carbs: 4g;

Protein: 5g

Banana Nut Cake

Prep Time: 35 minutes | **Serve:** 6

- 1 cup blanched finely ground almond flour
- 2 large eggs.
- ¼ cup unsalted butter; melted.
- ¼ cup full-fat sour cream.
- ¼ cup chopped walnuts
- ½ cup powdered erythritol
- 2 tbsp. ground golden flaxseed.
- 2 ½ tsp. banana extract.
- 1 tsp. Vanilla extract.
- 2 tsp. baking powder.
- ½ tsp. Ground cinnamon.

1.Take a large bowl, mix almond flour, erythritol, flaxseed, baking powder, and cinnamon. Stir in butter, banana extract, vanilla extract, and sour cream

2.Add eggs to the mixture and gently stir until fully combined. Stir in the walnuts

3.Pour into a 6-inch nonstick cake pan and place into the air fryer basket. Adjust the temperature to 300 Degrees F and set the timer for 25 minutes

4.Cake will be golden, and a toothpick inserted in the center will come out clean when fully cooked. Allow to fully cool to avoid crumbling.

Nutrition: Calories: 263; Protein: 7.6g; Fiber: 3.1g; Fat: 23.6g; Carbs: 18.4g

Olives and Kale

Prep Time: 25 minutes | **Serve:** 4

- 4 eggs; whisked

- 1 cup kale; chopped.

- ½ cup black olives, pitted and sliced

- 2 tbsp. cheddar; grated Cooking spray

- A pinch of salt and black pepper

1.Take a bowl and mix the eggs with the rest of the

ingredients except the cooking spray and whisk well.

2.Now, take a pan that fits in your air fryer and grease it

with the cooking spray, pour the olives mixture inside,

spread

3.Put the pan into the machine and cook at 360°F for 20

minutes. Serve for breakfast hot.

Nutrition: Calories: 220; Fat: 13g; Fiber: 4g; Carbs: 6g;

Protein: 12g

Cheesy Turkey

Prep Time: 30 minutes | **Serve:** 4

- 1 turkey breast, skinless, boneless; cut into strips and browned
- 2 cups almond milk
- 2 cups cheddar cheese; shredded
- 2 eggs; whisked
- 2 tsp. olive oil
- 1 tbsp. chives; chopped.
- Salt and black pepper to taste.

1.Take a bowl and mix the eggs with milk, cheese, salt, pepper, and the chives and whisk well.

2.Preheat the air fryer at 330°F, add the oil, heat it, add the turkey pieces and spread them well

3.Add the egg mixture, toss a bit, and cook for 25 minutes.

Nutrition: Calories: 244; Fat: 11g; Fiber: 4g; Carbs: 5g; Protein: 7g

Mushrooms and Cheese Spread

Prep Time: 25 minutes | **Serve:** 4

- ¼ cup mozzarella; shredded ½ cup coconut cream

- 1 cup white mushrooms

- A pinch of salt and black pepper Cooking spray

1.Put the mushrooms in your air fryer's basket, grease with cooking spray, and cook at 370°F for 20 minutes.

2.Transfer to a blender, add the remaining ingredients, pulse well, divide into bowls and serve as a spread.

Nutrition: Calories: 202; Fat: 12g; Fiber: 2g; Carbs: 5g; Protein: 7g

Cheesy Sausage Balls

Prep Time: 22 minutes | **Serve:** 16 balls

- 1 lb. pork breakfast sausage

- 1 large egg.

- 1 oz. full-fat cream cheese; softened.

- ½ cup shredded Cheddar cheese

1.Mix all ingredients in a large bowl. Form into sixteen (1-inch balls. Place the balls into the air fryer basket. Adjust the temperature to 400 Degrees F and set the timer for 12 minutes. Shake the basket two- or three-times during cooking

2.Sausage balls will be browned on the outside and have an internal temperature of at least 145 Degrees F when completely cooked.

Nutrition: Calories: 424; Protein: 22.8g; Fiber: 0.0g; Fat: 32.2g; Carbs: 1.6g

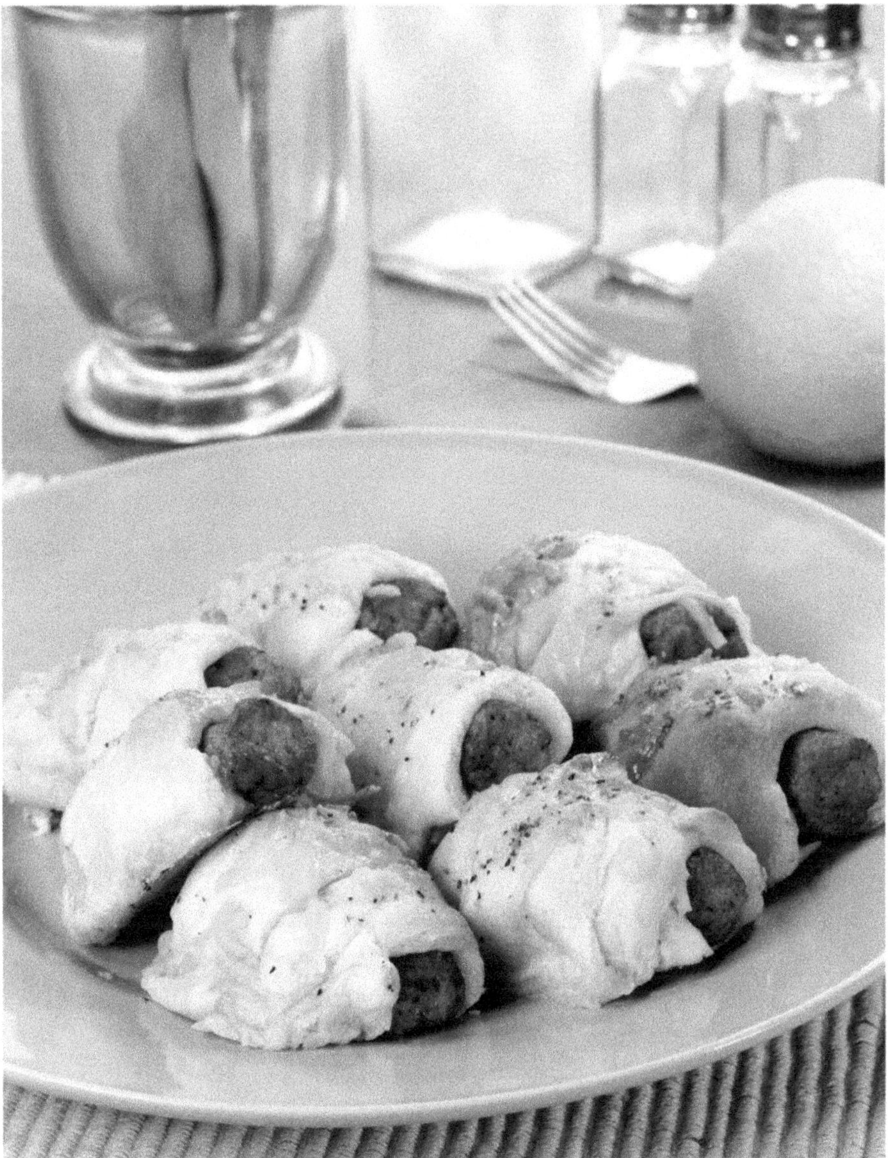

Lightning Source UK Ltd.
Milton Keynes UK
UKHW020807281022
411243UK00001B/16

9 781802 773347